A Non-Christian View of Jesus and Christianity

By Ali Zwaik

Copyright

A Non-Christian View of Jesus and Christianity

Subtitle: How the Non-Christian Believes in Jesus and Christianity

Copyright © 2013 by Ali Zwaik

ISBN-13: 978-1-939535-20-7

ISBN: 1939535204

E-Book ISBN-13: 978-1-939535-21-4

E-Book ISBN: 1939535212

www.deepseapublishing.com

Printed in the United States of America

Table of Contents

Introduction

The religious belief is a mobilizing force for a lot of the world's nations and peoples. For example, the adherents of Christianity, who represent a large portion of the human community as a whole is not less than 20% of earth's population.

Indeed, Christianity is amongst the most important and grand religions worldwide. It has a direct impact on people's whole life and economy. This big nation of adherents of Jesus, son of Mary, deals and interacts with all the human communities -- regardless of their diverse religions and creeds.

Decidedly, this connection, whether economic or social or even political, with Non-Christian communities has an effective impact, positively or negatively. Whatever these human communities have endeavored, they seem to ignore this sensitive and effective fact.

Obviously, all these nations, for their interest, should know how others think about their own religious beliefs and creeds so that they could be able to build-up more interdependent and realistic relationships with dogmatically differing nations. In fact, knowing how others ideologically and theologically think and conceive you as well as your doctrine, would open more clear and transparent horizons for the purpose of coexistence and convergence. In addition, the institutions and individuals could espouse easier ways to fulfill a constructive interchange with other nations of different creeds.

For these reasons, this interesting book has been compiled in order to understand each other's creed. It hopefully will also to contribute in normalizing the ties between nations of different religions with a view to find easier ways to frequent others.

Definitely, the religions and creeds of human communities are diverse and numerous. They sprawl around the Globe, which makes facts gathering and simplifying them to facilitate mutual human relationship an uneasy task.

This book will explain to the reader the non-Christian view of Christianity. It also show how they know and believe in Jesus. Indeed, I have collected the information from its main sources for the most of the great religions like Hinduism, Buddhism, Judaism, Paganism and Islam.

Furthermore, knowing others' creeds could provide you with a better chance for understanding and relating to the people of different creeds. And finally, it opens for you a new human outlook, which will be helpful for individuals, institutions and countries in order to set-up more pure and beneficial human links for all without violence or hatred.

The Family of Mary (Jesus' mother)

It is difficult to find specific or historical details about Mary's Family. Though the historical information available by various sources is not clear enough to give the real picture of that holy family, the only clear and specific information we can find is in the Islamic writings and documents.

The Islam Holy Book (the Quran) describes Jesus' mother's family with excellent and thoughtful words. The Quran showered this family with such special veneration and holiness to the degree, that it has a complete chapter devoted to Mary and her son Jesus. They named this chapter "the Family of Imran." Of its 114 chapters, it also has another chapter about Jesus' mother named "Marium" (Marium's Chapter). Marium is the Islamic name of Jesus mother.

Surely, the Family of Imran who begot Mary was bestowed a distinguished value which is not less than that given to Adam, Noah, and the Family of Abraham. And that is the veneration for this family who begot Mary, that has consequently begotten Jesus, and this veneration has not been given to any other human being as stated in Islamic documentations.

Mary's mother is a descendent of venerated family in the present life and in the hereafter. She also has been described with chastity and purity and all other noblest descriptions deserved for the best human. The Family of Mary (as it has been described in the Islamic holy book) enjoyed a grand reputation within the community in which she lived. People considered her impeccably credible in terms of what she said and good acts. She is also known as a philanthropic; especially in favor of the poor and paupers, with submission and God's love and worship.

Those distinguished attributives are given to the Family of Mary in the in the Noble Quran. The descriptive words in these chapters of the family have been well chosen in order to give a clear meaning of the characters of this family.

In history most of the documents about Mary described her dress similar to this picture.

(Picture painted by artist Warner Sallman. Titled: *Mary, Mother of Jesus.* See: http://www.christcenteredmall.com/stores/art/sallman/mary-mother-of-jesus.htm)

This is another example of a classic viewpoint of the
Virgin Mary, from San Lorenzo Church in Verona
Italy.
Titled*: Heart of the Virgin Mary.*

It is mentioned in the Holy Quran in the chapter of *The Family of Imran* verse 33 and 34 "God chose Adam and Noah and the family of Ibrahim and the family of Imran (Mary family) over all other beings…." This verse illustrates the extent of eminence of this family. God gave her the ability to interact well with people without fearing anyone. Mary worshipped, loved and continuously implored him to watch over all those she lived, loved, and encountered. She believed everyone should praise God and seek his guidance in all that they do.

One day Mary's mother felt that she is pregnant and she experienced happiness concerning this pregnancy. When she made sure of her pregnancy she supplicated and prayed her Lord and implored him to make her fetus a righteous human devoted exclusively, to be a devout worshipper of God the Creator, the All-Mighty. She implored her Lord so that her fetus will be devoted uniquely for God. She wanted the child to worship and consecrate himself to God. And she hopes God makes this child an upright man who helps, does good and is philanthropic. As Mary's mother prayed, she beseeched God to make this fetus solely devoted to his worship.

Days passed and Mary's mother and the family of Imran waited in expectation of the new born who will make the mother and the family happy. Indeed the promised day had come and Mary's mother underwent childbirth. The family of Imran got ready to receive her new born who will bring happiness to the mother and delight the family. Mary experienced easy childbirth and was told that her child was a female.

Mary's mother experienced sadness due to female being born, because in that time all people preferred the male rather than the female -- especially in terms of consecration and worship of God.

Mary's mother suffered a lot as a result of this and felt tense disappointment because her female baby would not be able to worship God as same as the male. Mary's mother, under these circumstances, reasoned these things as a simple human would without taking in consideration the will and powerfulness of God. But she soon realized this mistake and begged forgiveness of her Lord. She was saddened and objected to God's bestowal, while she realizes without doubt that God knows what he created and what she begot. She understood, that if God wanted her to beget a male he can make it so, but God decided notwithstanding.

She begged a pardon of God and told him that she begot a female who is unable to worship God as the male can; nevertheless God knew very well. She prayed God again so that he makes her daughter blessed born, obedient and philanthropic in favor of all people. She also asked him to safe keep her and her progeny from Satan's temptation who is truly man's foe. She supplicated God to thank him for the grace he endowed her and incarnated in her daughter, who she called eventually Mary. She is now Mary daughter of Imran. The Holy Book of Muslims (the Quran) stated in verses 35 and 36 in chapter of *The Family of Imran* that God said "Remember when the wife of Imran said, 'My Lord, I have pledged to you what is in my womb, devoting to Your service. Please accept my prayer

.You are the All-Hearing, the All-Knowing.' When she gave birth, she said, 'My Lord !I have given birth to a girl.' God knew very well what she had given birth to, male and female are not the same. '…and I have named her Mary and placed her and her children your safekeeping from the accursed Satan.'"

Mary Grew up and became a beautiful and polite person who enjoys excellent manners and good conduct with all people. Mary had been under the fostering of Zachariah -- safe and secure loved by people and she had love them. She had been spending her time in prayer, invoking God and worshipping him.

One day Zachariah went into Mary's shelter and found her praying in the place she dedicated for prayer and God's invocation. He was surprised to find foods and sweet fruits that are not usual in this society. Astonished, Zachariah asked her, "O Mary, who provides you with this food and nice fruits? I am surprised to find this food without knowing who brings to you." Mary smiled and said "My Sir, this is from my Lord who is solely provides for all creatures; in fact, he is the All-Provider -- the All-Knowing."[1]

---

[1] The Holy Book of Muslims (The Quran) described this happening in the verse 37 from the chapter Mary saying "Every time Zachariah visited her in the Upper room, he found food with her. He said, 'Mary, how did you come by this?' She said, 'It is from God. God provides for whoever He wills without any reckoning.'"

Mary's Dialogue with Angels

During an extraordinary moment of fate, while she was sitting in full serenity and tranquility, she heard a beautiful voice calling her out by her name, Mary. She became frightened, but still listened carefully to this voice even though she did not see anybody. After short while, she calmed down and soon realized that it was a voice she enjoyed listening to. The speaker told her that he is God's herald, an Angel's voice sent to her by God. The angelic voice told Mary as stated in the Holy Book of Muslims (the Quran), "O Mary, God gives you good news because God has chosen you over all other world women, so obey and pray your lord continuously."[2]

Mary was reassured after her discussion with the angels. She was extremely happy because she knew God loved her. Consequently she intensified her worship and consecration of God the Unique, the One, in praying, good doing and righteousness.

---

[2] The Holy Book of Muslims (the Quran) provides the discussion held between Mary and the angel in verse 42. "And when angels said, 'Mary, God has chosen you and purified you. He has chosen you over all other women. Mary, obey your Lord and prostrate and bow with those who bow.'"))

Annunciation of Virgin Mary

The first discussion between Mary and the angels was short. Sometime later, she heard angelic voice that she accustomed to hear calling her again. She remained tranquil this time, and she did not become scared or afraid as before. There is no reason to be scared. She knew that the Angel's voice was calling her to a business that concerns her and all mankind. Although, this time the angel's voice was more troublesome to Mary. It was not as it was previous time. She got upset due to the fact that she did not expect the orders she received from angels. What she heard is a sort of thing which is beyond human comprehension capacity and his intellectual and mental ability. Mary was merely a human being that God had selected to accomplish a hard task.

The angels said to Mary, in a speech characterized by gladness and delight from the side of angels, "Mary, God gives you good news that you will give birth to child his name is the Messiah son of Mary."

He will be a son of high esteem while young and when he is mature. God made him pure and he will be a great prophet. God will give him the Gospel.

Mary was astonished by what she heard from the Angel and asked, "How can I possibly have a son without being married, or committing any sin?" The Angel responded to her quietly that God, when he wills it, can create or do anything he says or wishes to be. Thus, he will create Jesus, son of Mary, without father as he created Adam of earth. God is All-Mighty.

Verily, Mary daughter of Imran (Jesus' mother) presumably, has been undoubtedly created to be the ideal of humanity in terms of endurance during difficult conditions.

She had never been a skeptic of God or his powerfulness. Truly, she worshipped God faithfully during even the worst of times. She impeccably put her trust in God despite these very difficult conditions she had faced, thanks to her achieving a high degree of transparency and faith.

All this despite the fact that the human mind is of limited capacities and unable to understand himself, incapable also to safeguard himself from perdition.

Furthermore, what she heard from angels is incredible for ordinary human mind; suggesting to her that she will give birth to a matchless child within humanity as whole. This is an extraordinary thing but Mary's belief in God's Will made her committed to this. In order to face this situation, she withdrew from her people. She retreated to an eastern place from her home at Zachariah's house, and veiled herself from people so that they could not see or talk to her.

She established herself solely in this place far from her family in expectation of what surprises that may come.

Mary conceived Jesus, by God's decree, while being virgin -- chaste, pure and with devoted to loving God. In addition, she endured hardships and fear because she knows how human beings think. The man, whose mind is partially possessed by Satan, has a tendency to accuse and tempt rather than rectify or exculpate. As time passes, Mary's worry increases in her secluded retreat. Her isolation from people increases her anticipation of that tremendous and great day -- the day when she will give birth to her son Jesus. The duration of Jesus conception lasted like ordinary man until the time of his birth. That promised day witnessed the coming and the birth of the most august human on the earth, from a mother's womb. A mother who couldn't possibly imagine or expect it as the unprecedented and unrepeated divine miracle of human history.

Mary suffered as any women from throe with its pains and fatigue. Nonetheless, her belief in God's destiny alleviated it for her. Speaking about Mary during these critical moments, as mentioned in the Holy Book of Muslims (the Quran), will make the submissive people impressed and they will experience the feeling of pity in favor of Mary because she had said: "If only I had died before this time and was something discarded and forgotten."

The Holy Book of Muslims (the Quran) stated the details of this dramatic scenario and emotionally narrated the great importance of this event as cited from the verse (16) until the verse (23) of the chapter of Mary. "(17) So she took a veil (to screen herself) from them; then We sent to her Our spirit, and there appeared to her a well-made man. (18) Mary said, "Would that the Beneficent God would protect me from you. Leave me alone if you are a God fearing person". (19) "Nay, I am only a messenger from thy Lord, (to announce) to thee the gift of a holy son. (20) She said: "How shall I have a son, seeing that no man has touched me, and I am not unchaste?" (21) He said: So (it will be). Thy Lord saith: It is easy for Me. And (it will be) that We may make of him a revelation for mankind and a mercy from Us, and it is a thing ordained. (22) She conceived the child and retreated with him to a distant and solitary place. (23) And the throes (of childbirth) compelled her to betake herself to the trunk of a palm tree. She said: Oh, would that I had died before this, and had been a thing quite forgotten!"

Jesus' Birth

When labor's pains aggravated Mary, she headed to distant place from her home, in orchard of date-palms and sit down under one blessed date-palm, which will witness the birth of the most august creature under its leafs, and shadows him with its shade. Mary sat down under that date-palm till she gave birth to Jesus and admired by this lovely august born. She took care of him as any mother, but worried when she considered bringing him to her home and what people will say.

In these critical circumstances, troubled Mary worried she would be unable to make decision and she did not know what to do. Her boy told her "Don't be sad nor afraid, God decreed for you all benediction and dignity." Then he asked her to shake trunk of date-palm so that sweet dates drop to her and said, "Eat and drink and look at me. You will not get bored of watching me." He also advised her when she goes back to home that she mustn't talk to anybody. Inform them that you are fasting for God.

The great lady, the mother of Jesus, carried her son between her hands and faced fearlessly what people would say because she was certain about her son Jesus and the fateful fact decreed by the Creator of the Universe. Once she reached her village, the people set to insult and reproached her -- qualifying her with inappropriate words against her and against her august son. But she excused

Church of the Nativity
(Built in 327 A.D. in Bethlehem. It is traditionally
believed to be the birthplace of Jesus)

them because they were people who know not. Mary's deed
was increasingly criticized by many well-known people of the
villages. As cited in the Holy Book of Muslims, these
important but ignorant people would say, "Oh Mary! How
do you allow yourself to commit this act while you are a sister
of an upright man and your mother is a chaste woman, your
brother Aaron is honest and devoted to God, how did you
this?"

When people's talk reached this extent of vehemence and insults, she quietly said to them, "Oh people, talk to my son, Jesus son of Mary." People laughed at her and mocked of her say and said, "How can we talk to one baby whose age did not exceed one day? Then the baby rose his head from hands of his mother before their sight and said in a clear voice heard by all attendance around him, "Oh people, I am Jesus of Mary. God created me and given me the Science and the Book, and made me a Prophet and his Messenger to you and to the coming generations. He also blesses me wherever I am. He ordained me to perform the prayer and exclusively dedicate the worshipping to him. Verily, he is my Creator and the Creator of everything." Jesus added, "Verily, God is my One and Only Lord, and he is your Lord."

"He commanded me to respect and love my mother. Also to pray and pay alms and give to the poor as long as I live." Jesus also told them God did not make him a violent nor evil-doer tyrant. He said peace and love will be upon me from my birth until my death, and when I am resurrected and live again.

The Holy Book of Muslims (the Quran) clearly tells this remarkable story in the chapter of *Mary* from the verse 24. Then she heard the baby saying, "Do not be sad. Your Lord has caused a stream to run at your feet. If you shake the trunk of the palm tree, it will provide you with fresh ripe dates. Eat, drink, and rejoice. Should you see a person going by, tell him that on this day you have promised the Beneficent God to fast and never talk to any human being." She took him to her people and they said, "Mary, this is indeed an strange thing. "O sister of Aaron! Thy father was not a man of evil, nor thy mother a woman unchaste!" She pointed to the baby (and referred them to him for their answer). They said, "How can we talk to a baby in the cradle?" He said, "I am the servant of God. He has given me the Book and has appointed me to be a Prophet. And He has made me blessed wherever I may be, and He has enjoined on me prayer and poor-rate so long as I live. He has commanded me to be good to my parents and has not made me an arrogant rebellious person. And peace on me on the day I was born, and on the day I die, and on the day I am raised to life." Such was the true story of Jesus, the son of Mary, about which they dispute bitterly.

Jesus was born in Bethlehem. It is a town in Palestine in a location currently called Nativity Church. He was born during the era of the roman emperor Augustus, who ruled when Palestine was administered by the Roman Governor, Herodotus. Herodotus, who was elected as the Governor over the land of Sham at that time the Jews, learnt of the birth of Jesus. The news of his birth spread over the country asserting that this boy, given birth by Mary the daughter of Imran while she was a virgin, will have great influence over the people and will put the Roman Empire in peril. Thus, King Herodotus gave an order to kill any first born boy in Palestine in order to neutralize any threat from this newborn.

Mary found out the matter, so she decided to hide Jesus, and she chose a quiet time and left Nazareth and headed Egypt. She stayed in Egypt until the death of the Herodotus. Then she came back with Jesus in the company of her husband, Joseph the carpenter. Jesus was seven years of age at that time. Mary lived in the Christian city of Nazareth, which is found in the province of Palestine. When

Jesus reached twelve years she headed with her son to Jerusalem, which in Arabic is called "Al-Quds or Aur Salem," while in Hebraic is called " Aurshalim." Jesus began his life worshipping God following Moses model as stated in the Torah.

The historians indicated that Jesus was born around one thousand and four hundred years after the birth of Moses.

His Message (Jesus' Message)

Jesus lived with his mother in the town of Nazareth after their return from Egypt, in tranquility and serenity while praising God and praying to him without boredom. Subjects of the society in which Jesus lived were mostly children of Israel and followers of Moses epistle since 1400 years ago. Over the centuries from Moses time, many of Moses adepts went astray from the right path elucidated by Moses. Meanwhile, Jesus and his mother were watching the perversions that adepts of Moses message were committing, including their different races like Canaanite Arabs and the children of Israel, and others. Thus, Jesus and his mother were saddening by these deviations and arrogant challenges against God. They were observing children of Israel committing sins and prohibitions and recidivating without shame or fearing God.

The Holy Book of Muslims (the Quran) described clearly the situation of the adepts of **Moses** during Jesus era and before revelation of his Message. "Those among the tribe of Israel who disbelieve were cursed on the tongue of David and that of Jesus, son of Mary. This is because they rebelled and overstepped the limits." This is the situation of Jesus people before the revelation of the Message to him.

When he reached thirty years of age, Jesus went to meet John, son of Zachariah, who had been a prophet to his people. The prophet John baptized Jesus and blessed his devotion and worship of God. Jesus remarked that his people had forgotten or ignored the Message of Moses. He wished they would return to the worship and glorification of God and turn their back on sin.

Jesus was thirty years old when the divine inspiration was sent down to him via Inspiration Angel.

God advised Jesus that his message to children of Israel should be aimed at driving them to the straight path incarnated in Moses message and its teachings, which they had long ago abandoned. God told him, via the inspiration revealed to him, that his message is titled "the Bible" whilst the Moses message bears the name of "the Torah."

The Bible is God's Book and Words revealed to Jesus. It contains a religious law for everyday life, including God's worship and devotion guide.

Jesus had been instructed to start the preaching to his people, the children of Israel. They were to follow him and avoid sin and acts of immorality. Jesus taught them that Jesus and Moses are merely God's messengers chosen by God the Unique.

After the message was sent down to Jesus and after he was given permission by his Lord, Jesus invited children of Israel to follow him. He told them that his message is a close extension of Moses message. As cited in the Holy Book of Muslims (the Quran) in the chapter of *The Ranks*: "And when Jesus son Mary said, 'O Children of Israel! I am the Messenger of God into you, confirming that which was (revealed) before me in the Torah and giving you the good news of a Messenger after me whose name is Ahmed.' When he brought them the Clear Signs, they said, 'This is downright magic.'"

Children of Israel accused Jesus of witchcraft and disagreed and disobeyed him. But Jesus continued calling the children of Israel to follow him and forbid the wrong deeds they were committing. Jesus pursued his calling, day and night, in order to guide them.

He had been trying to make the people understand what had been forbidden for them, that his message and Moses message are the same, and that both were dictated by the Lord of the Universe, the Creator of both Jesus and Moses. The messages of God are sent down in different times and in accordance with conditions of society at the time. The Holy Book of Muslims (the Quran) stated in the verse 58 of the chapter of the family of Imran ((I come confirming the Torah I find already there, and to make lawful for you some of what was previously forbidden to you that is a straight path."))

A lot of Canaanite Arabs and a great number of tribes of Israel believed in Jesus -- especially tribes of the disciples. However, many of the other tribes of Israel arrogantly disbelieved, and accused Jesus of dealing with sorcery. They persisted in their disbelief and refused to follow Jesus, and moreover, they plotted to liquidate him and undermine his Message.

Jesus felt that the Jewish disbelievers will never respond him. The disbelievers decided not to follow him or respect his Message. He had displayed miracles from God to persuade them about the veracity of his Message. Jesus hoped the Signs and Powers of God would reinforce the message, but they still refused to follow him even when seeing with their own eyes.

Jesus Miracles as stated in the Quran (The Islam's Holy Book)

Jesus, son of Mary, was since his creation and conception, a real miracle because he had spoken to people in just a few hours of his birth. He confirmed the chastity and guiltlessness of Mary. And he informed them that Jesus, son of Mary, was created by God from a mother only -- without a father.

That was his first and greatest miracle, but the arrogance of Israelite disbelievers ignored that sublime miracle and all other facts. As stated in the Holy Book of Muslims (the Quran) in the verse 156 of the chapter of *The Women*, "and because of their disbelief and of their speaking against Mary a tremendous calumny."

In addition, their rancor accentuated against Jesus and they tried to incapacitate him and destroy his message. In fact, they were weaved plots asking him repeatedly for more miracles, and incredible and inconceivable things to embarrass him and make people think that he is merely a magician. But Jesus, whose God-given strength and miracles had shown all Israelites decisive proof that he was a Messenger of God's Word to the people, was also sent for the well-being of humanity as a whole. He was sent to establish a new way of life that was more suited to people, but still agreed with Moses message which lasted 1400 years.

In fact, the Bible is Jesus message, which is an extension of Moses message, which at that time, is perfect and appropriate for people's life. It is mentioned clearly in the Holy Book of Muslims (the Quran) when God said about Moses and Jesus messages in the verse 48 of the chapter *The Family of Imran* "He will teach him the Book and Wisdom, and the Torah and the Bible" and in the verse 50 of the same chapter, "I come confirming the Torah I find already there, and to make lawful for you some of what was previously forbidden to you."

The Israelites disbelieved in Jesus and his message insisting that they will not follow him until he show them the miracles God gave him, and they intentionally ignored the extraordinary story of his creation and birth.

As a result, God had - as a refutation of God's enemies allegations and fortifying Jesus - given Jesus the power to make miracles that was not given to another human. His miracles were as follows:

1-   He brings forth the dead by God's permission;
2-   He creates a bird-shape out of clay and then he breathes into it and it became a living bird by God's permission;
3-   He heals the blind and the leper by God's permission;
4-   He sends food down from heaven to them by God's permission.

God gave Jesus these powers to be a conclusive proof he was a prophet and had a superior connection with God. But the Israelites became arrogant and rejected Jesus' call despite the fact that they knew the authenticity of his message. Indeed, the Holy Book of Muslims (the Quran) stated, in a very well-spoken and magnificent linguistic style, God's exclusively given miracles to Jesus in the verse 48 of the chapter of *The Family of Imran* "and he will teach him the Scripture and Wisdom and the Torah and the Gospel."

Jesus gave life to the dead by permission of God. Once, an Israelite who was amongst Jesus disciples, was killed unjustly. The others in the community refused to reveal who had murdered the man. While Jesus knew with certitude the murderer, Jesus asked the people to disclose and testify in favor of the dead man. But all the people refused to testify with respect to his murder. One man mocked Jesus saying that the true witness of murder is the murdered himself. Of course, that is impossible.

Jesus said let us go to his grave and ask him about his assassin and ask God to revive him so that he testifies before us. The people and Jesus headed to the grave of the murdered man. They all doubted Jesus' ability to resurrect a dead man. Jesus stood up beside the grave and prayed to his Lord, and asked him to resurrect the buried. The people remained completely silent, afraid and surprised.

The grandiose and unexpected moment came by permission of God the Creator of the Universe, and before the Israelites. Then grave was opened before their eyes and the man in question got out, delighted to see Jesus and his companions present. Then Jesus asked the man who had killed him, and the man told Jesus the name of the murderer. The people heard the testimony of the victim and Jesus asked God to render him back into his grave as he was.

This is Jesus, son of Mary, who resurrected the dead by permission of God, the miracle that had not given to anybody else before.

A Table Spread With food From Heaven

Some tribes of Israel, who were hostile to Jesus and doubted in his proclaimed messenger and prophet status did not believe in him – despite miracles and signs they saw. They continued defying Jesus asking him for more grandiose miracles only to incapacitate Jesus. The disbelievers wanted to make people think that he is unable to satisfy their unimaginable demands. One of Jesus's hostile persons said that we should plan or scheme new ways to prove his inability to validate his prophethood. They needed to do everything possible to question his abilities and prove that he has no connection with God. Furthermore, they should assert that what he is doing is merely a magic. They wanted him to send down a table spread with food from heaven. They wanted to see this table during its descent from heaven. They expected that this table will be full of many kinds of sweet foods so that all attendance may eat.

They ascertained that if Jesus succeeded in sending down this table in question they will believe and follow him.

Jesus was surprised at this demand telling them, "You did not already believe in me yet, despite what I performed and have shown to you by permission of God." But their answer was eminently resourceful saying to him, "Of course, we believe in you as God's messenger but we desire to make sure of that. And as soon as the table descends from heaven we will be sure that you fulfilled your promise and we will follow you and we will never disobey you. Also sending down this table will be as feast for us."

Jesus said it will be sent down for you and he fixed the appointment in order that all people see this grandiose event in the history of Israelite people.

People gathered for this great and extraordinary happening, and Jesus led the people and prayed to his Lord. He asked the Lord to send down a table spread with food. It will be a feast for Israelite people and their progeny over the lifetime.

Angels told Jesus to be reassured that God will send it down shortly. Soon the people saw the table descending from heaven spread with all kinds of sweet foods they requested. After the table sent down many of the Israelites believed in Jesus as God's messenger and submitted in following and obeying his orders.

But a minority of arrogant Israelites persisted in their disbelief, hatred and rancor against Jesus despite all miracles Jesus had shown. This group of Jews remained disbelievers in Jesus until now.

The holy book of Muslim (the Quran) accurately described the event of the descending table in an interesting linguistic style. Furthermore, in the Quran there is a complete chapter named "the Chapter of the Table" dedicated to this marvelous story among other facts. In that chapter the event was described as an absolute miracle.

The Holy Book of Muslims (the Quran) stated, describing the sending down of the table from heaven to gain the favor of Israelites ((When the disciples said: O Jesus, son of Mary! is the Lord able to send down for us a table spread with food from heaven? He said: Observe your duty to God, if you are true believers. They said: We wish to eat thereof, that we may satisfy our hearts and know that you told us the truth and to be among those who witness it. Jesus, son of Mary, said: O God, Lord of us, send down for us a table spread with food from heaven, that it may be a feast for us, for the first of us, and for the last of us, and a sign from you. Give us sustenance, you are the Best of Sustainers. God said: I will send it down to you but if anyone among you disbelieves after that, I will punish him with a punishment the like of which I will not inflict on anyone else in all the worlds!))

The Completion of his Message, His Pretended Death – His Ascent to God?

Jesus lived, according to available and cited historical documents and information, thirty three years. Three of those years were known as the Message Revelation (the Bible).

The Message period begins with the revelation by God to Jesus until the end. For Muslims, the Bible means God's book and words reveled to Jesus. It includes all the guidance that man needs towards spending a tranquil life as God chose it, especially in terms of worshipping God, doing good deeds, avoiding sins, and organizing one's life in general. In fact, the Bible is a sacred book for Muslims as is the Holy Quran.

A lot of Israelites persisted in disobeying Jesus and qualified him as a magician. Many also described his mother with manner which is not appropriate to the woman God chose and selected among the entire world's women.

Some tribes of Israel persisted in their disbelief, disobedience, and hostilities against Jesus, whilst other tribes of Israel believed and followed his Message. One of the main Israelite tribes who believed and obeyed Jesus was the tribe of the Disciples.

It is the disciples who supported and believed Jesus. They also backed him against his enemies. In addition, a lot of the Canaanite tribes, populations of Sham land, believed in Jesus. Those Canaanites were Arab tribes at that time.

The Israelite foes of Jesus planned to eliminate him. Their creed and statue in the community were being challenged by Jesus' existence. When Jesus felt their hatred against him and discovered their plots, he decided to leave Nazareth and to travel to Jerusalem. He arrived at Jerusalem and was welcomed by its Israelite and Arab populations, who gathered around him listening to all that he said. Jesus' sermons displeased the Israelites Rabbis and his enemies from Rome, who finally decided to liquidate him.

The rulers of Roman Empire thought Jesus jeopardized their supremacy. He caused them many sleepless nights because they were afraid his extraordinary abilities may eventually weaken the power of the Roman Empire in the region. The common interest of Jesus' Israelite enemies and the Romans united them, and they decided to get rid of Jesus.

Some Israelite enemies of Jesus coordinated with the Roman King Pilate (Who is the king that succeeded the Roman King Herodotus after his death) and decide to kill him.

The Israelite foes of Jesus who are the allies of Roman ruler, started to look for Jesus everywhere to arrest and kill him. The Roman king also charged one of the enemies of Jesus to bring him to trial as soon as he is arrested, and to issue a death by crucifixion sentence against him.

Some documents state that one of Jesus' foes from the Israelites, so-called Judas Iscariot, was leading an active search to arrest Jesus and extradite him to the Roman King in order to kill him. According to versions of these documents, Jesus was arrested by his trackers and extradited to the Romans. After the declaration of his death and crucifixion sentence, Judas Iscariot disappeared and never found after Jesus arrest.

The Holy Book of Muslims (the Quran) has clarified the details of the alleged Jesus killing. And among the main facts are that when his enemies came to arrest him, they were led by Judas Iscariot. God, however, immediately took Jesus up to him alive, safe and sound. Then God transformed Judas Iscariot's appearance to that of Jesus. The people arrested Judas, believing that he was Jesus. God made him take Jesus' place, and was tortured and crucified as punishment in the present life and the hereafter.

The Muslims do not believe in the killing and crucifying of Jesus. They believe that God safeguarded and lifted him sound and safe. Moreover, some books of the interpretation of the Quran stated that Jesus will be back at the end of the time. This is the belief of the majority of Muslims.

Muslims believe fully that God is the One God, the All-Mighty, who would never allow the disbelieving enemies of Jesus to arrest and torture him. Instead God lifted Jesus in all dignity and honor. On the contrary, it is his enemies who were tortured crucified.

The belief of Muslims that Jesus never killed or crucified is a logical interpretation, as stories of all prophets and Messengers cited in the Quran, the Torah and the Bible (like Abraham, Noah, Moses, Saleh, Idriss, and others, may peace upon them) had not been held by their enemies nor killed. The Holy Book of Muslims (the Quran) supplied many facts on Jesus and his non-crucifixion and non-killing as cited in the verse 25 from the chapter of the Creator ((And if deny you, those before them also denied. Their messengers came into them with clear proofs (of God's sovereignty, and with the Psalms and the Scripture giving light)).

Also, God said in the verse 55 of the chapter of the Family of Imran ((When God said "Jesus, I will take you back and raise you up to Me, and purify you of those who disbelieve. And I will place the people who follow you above those who disbelieve until the Day of Rising. Then you will all return to Me, and I will judge between you regarding the things about which you differed.))

The Quran confirmed that man who was crucified was not Jesus, but his likeness. As stated in the Quran, verse 157, the chapter of the Women ((And their saying ,"We killed the Messiah, Jesus son of Mary, Messenger of God. They did not kill him and they did not crucify him but it was made to seem so to him. Those who argue about him are in doubt about it. They have no real knowledge of it, just conjecture. But certainly did not kill him. God raised him up to Himself. God is Almighty, All-Wise.))

God said in the Holy Book of Muslims that the true disciples of Jesus are compassionate and are of the highest humanistic quality, and whom he admonished to not deviate from the path of worshipping God. As he said in the verse 27 from the chapter of the Iron ((Then We sent Our messengers following in their footsteps and sent "Jesus son of Mary after them, giving him the Gospel. We put compassion and mercy in the hearts of those who followed him. They invented monasticism – We did not prescribe it for them – purely out of desire to gain the pleasure of God, but even so they did not observe it as it should have been observed. To those of them who believed We gave their reward but many of them are deviators.))

God has warned, via the Quran, the disciples of Jesus against committing Polytheism. Inviting them instead to believe in the One God, the Unique who is the First and the Last, the Creator of the Universe. This dialogue is narrated in the Quran in the verse 116 from the chapter of the Table ((and when God says "Jesus son of Mary! Did you say to people, take me and my mother as gods besides God?" He will say, "Glory be to you! It is not for me to say what I have no right to say! If I had said it, then you would have known it. You know what is in myself but I do not know what is in yourself. You are the Knower of all unseen things. I said to them nothing but what You ordered me to say: "Worship God, my Lord and your Lord." I was a witness against them as long as I remained among them, but when you took me back to You, you were the One watching over them. You are Witness of all things."

Indeed, Islam venerated Jesus, son of Mary, and granted him a pure and august image. He deserves this image as the belief in Jesus Message and in the chastity of his mother is primordial in the Islamic creed and religion. Therefore, the Holy Book of Muslims has repeated the name of Jesus 25 times whilst the name of Muhammad is directly cited 5 times.

Muslims believe undoubtedly in the birth of Jesus from a virgin mother and Jesus is of God's spirit and was created by God's Word without a father. They also they believe that God endowed Jesus with miracles not given to any other messengers. For Muslims loving Jesus is equal to loving Muhammad, as stated in the Quran in the verse 284 from the chapter of the Cow. ((The messenger believes in what has been sent down to him from his Lord, and so do the believers. Each one believes in God his angels and His books and His messengers. We do not differentiate between any of His Messengers.)).

The Holy Book of Muslims and the Islamic religion which venerates Jesus and his mother to this extent deserve to be respected by Jesus followers and respect its Messenger Muhammad and his followers and dialogue with them on differences in order to satisfy God and protect the interest of all.

Old Testament (Moses)

Moses was born in Egypt about 1450 BC. His name is stated 136 times in the Quran. His full name: Moses son of Azer son of Law son of Jacob son of Isaac son of Abraham. He had been sent to the Pharaoh's people in Egypt. The Quran qualified Pharaoh as despotic tyrant who exceedingly allowed himself and his clan everything.

God described Pharaoh's tyranny and despotism in the Quran as cited in the chapter of the Story, verse 4 ((Pharaoh exalted himself arrogantly in the land and divided its people into camps ,oppressing one group of them by slaughtering their sons and letting their women live. He was one of the corrupters)). In fact, Pharaoh exceedingly oppressed the people of Egypt and the Israelites. In addition, he was arrogant and behaved as he is god on the earth.

The story of Moses and the Pharaoh began with Moses' birth. A cassock told Pharaoh, interpreting the Pharaoh's dream, that an Israelite boy will be born and he will witness the destruction of the Pharaoh's kingdom.

After Pharaoh heard the cassock's speech he immediately made the decision to kill each male born in his kingdom in order to avoid this danger revealed by the cassock. The news of the killing of newborns propagated in the country and Moses' mother heard of it. As a result, she hid her boy Moses. But she got scared for Moses life, and she began thinking of what to do in order keep her boy safe. Thus divine will intervened and inspired Moses' mother to make woody box. She put Moses inside and placed it on the river. The river level changed and the wooden box floated downstream until it reached the Pharaoh's palace façade. The Pharaoh's wife, who was sitting near the river's edge, saw that floating box. She ordered her guards to bring that floating box and she opened it and found nice smiling boy. She took him into the palace, and decided to hide him from people eyes. She was sterile, and when the Pharaoh came upon her, she informed him of the boy. She implored the Pharaoh to not kill boy, because she want adopt him as her son without people's knowledge.

Eventually, Pharaoh accepted the boy for his wife's sake. As a result, Moses the baby remained in Pharaoh Palace, and as God's compassion towards Moses mother, the baby refused the breastfeeding from all women. Meanwhile, Moses sister knew the news that the baby refused the breastfeeding of all women. She went to Pharaoh's wife and told her that she knows a woman who is able to breastfeed him. She did not reveal her identity, nor the identity of Moses' mother. Immediately, the Pharaoh's wife consented and Moses returned, by God's will, to his mother. She feels very happy, is reassured of her faith, and gives thanks to God. The Quran narrated this happening in the chapter of the Story, from verse seven, God said ((We revealed to Moses's mother, "Suckle him and then when you fear for him cast him into the sea do not fear or grieve. We will return him to you and make him one of the messengers." The family of Pharaoh picked him up so that he might be an enemy and a source of grief to them. Certainly Pharaoh and Haman and their troops were in the wrong. The wife of Pharaoh said, "A source of delight for me and for you, do not kill him. It may well be that he will be of use to user perhaps we could adopt him as a son." They were not aware.)) And in verse 12, from the same chapter ((We first made him refuse all wet-nurses, so she said "shall I show you to household who will feed him for you and be good to him? That how We returned him to his mother so that she might delight her eyes and feel no grief and so that she would know that God's promise is true. But most of them do not know this.))

Moses lived under foster care of the Pharaoh Palace until he became a nice, robust man of good and noble ethics. One day he was walking down a town street, when he heard a cry for help by one of his compatriots fighting with a Coptic man. Moses went quickly to rescue his compatriot, and hit the Coptic man. The Coptic man died as a result of the blow. It was not premeditated murder; Moses did not mean to kill the man.

But Moses realized that he made an enormous mistake and he ought not have kill that man. He became frightened that Coptic man's family and friends might seek revenge, and set out to disappear to avoid being punished.

The Quran stated this story so that it will be a guide for all mankind in terms of unpremeditated murder. God ordained to not commit it under any condition. It is cited in the verse 14 of the chapter of the Story ((And when he reached his full strength and maturity, We gave him judgment and knowledge. That is how We recompense good-doers. He entered the city at a time when its inhabitants were unaware and found two men fighting there –one from his party and the other from his enemy. The one from his party asked for his support against the other from his enemy. So Moses hit him, dealing him a fatal blow. He said," This is part of Satan's handiwork. He truly is an outright and misleading enemy." He said, "My Lord, I have wronged myself. Forgive me." So He forgave him. He is the Ever-Forgiving, the Most Merciful.))

Moses decided to leave the town after one of his friends advised him to leave because people were searching for him to kill him. Moses left the town as a fugitive and afraid. He headed to an area called Median, a district area in Sinai desert. He walked within this deserted porous drought arid desert, in tranquility because he undoubtedly believes that God will help him concerning this dilemma. He walked day and night until he arrived at one of wells. He found a lot people busy watering their livestock. He sat down under the shadow of a tree and watched those people crowding over well and water. Among them the strong do not care of the weak. Meanwhile, he saw two women having difficulty watering their sheep due. As the strong do not allow the weak in the crowd to approach the well, he observed those women were waiting for the crowding to end. Since they could not get close, they looked for somebody who could help them in watering their sheep. But none of the crowd was helping them. Moses intervened and watered the sheep of those two women after asking them politely to do this for them, they appreciated that and Moses finished watering their sheep. They left and Moses came back to the tree's shadow and waited for God's rescue. After a short time he saw one of the women he had helped come in a chastely and polite manner up to him. She tells him that her father, who was an old man, invites him come to his house to reward you for your good deed. Moses accepted the invitation of the old man and went to meet him.

Moses came to old man and greeted him. The old man welcomed Moses in his house. Moses told him his story with the Pharaoh's people and difficulties of his leaving his homeland Egypt as a fugitive. The old man listened to the story and realized that this man he was either a great man or prophet. He told Moses to be assured that he is safe here and they will not reach you. The daughters of old man asked their father to employ this honest and robust man. The old man made this offer to Moses to be his sheepherder for period of nine years. And after which, he could marry one of his daughters. Moses accepted and became a member of the family doing his work in honest and committed manner until he completed the agreed period.

Moses intended to return to Egypt, and he prepared himself and his family for their journey to Egypt. He made his way through the Sinai desert, traveling during day and night in this vast and unpopulated desert. Moses and his family passed alongside a mountain in Sinai desert called Tur Mountain. During the night, Moses looked at mountain and began thinking about the greatness of God in his creatures.

Moses suddenly saw the light of a fire near the mountain. He was happy when he saw the fire near the mountain, thinking that there must be some herders or desert inhabitants. The night was very cold, and he needed a fire to warm his family. So he commanded his family to wait until he returns from the mountain with fire. He went to the place of that fire in order to get help from those people and bring some brand of it to set fire for warming.

It was not a long trip, but it was the greatest travel man ever made on the earth. Moses went to the mountain to bring fire, but he found himself in dialogue with God. No human had ever had such a conversation. He approached the fire, but he did not see anyone. But he did hear a voice talking to him. It is God's voice, the Al-Mighty telling to Moses: "O Moses it is I am God, I am your Lord take off your sandals you are in the Holy Valley."

Surprised, Moses trembled. But he retained himself and took off his sandals and he looked at the sky. Maybe he would hear more of God's plan.

Dialogue between God and Moses at Mount Sinai

This story is stated in the Quran in the chapter Taha, verse 9 till verse 81. ((Has the story of Moses not reached you? When he saw a fire and said to his family, "Wait here. I can make out a fire. Maybe I will bring you a brand from it, or will find guidance there." Then when he reached it, a voice called out, Moses! I am your Lord. Take off your sandals. You are in the holy valley of Tuwa. I have chosen you, so listen well to what is revealed. I am God. There is no god but Me, so worship Me and establish the prayer to remember Me. The Hour is coming but I have concealed it so that every self may be repaid for its efforts. Do not let those do not believe in it and follow their whims and desires debar from it or you will be destroyed. What is that in your right hand, Moses? He said "it is my staff. I lean on it and beat down leaves for my sheep with it and I have other uses for it." He said, "Throw it down, Moses." He threw it down and suddenly it was a slithering snake. He said "Take hold of it and have no fear. We will return it to its original form. Put your hand under your arm and press it to your side. It will emerge pure white yet quite unharmed, another sign. In this way We show you some of Our greatest Signs. Go to Pharaoh. He has overstepped the bounds. He said "O my Lord, expand my breast for me and make my task easy for me. Loosen the knot in my tongue so that they will understand my words. Assign me a helper from my family my brother Aaron. Strengthen my back by him and let him share in my task, so that we may glorify You much and remember You much, for You are watching us.")) Moses listened to his Lord's words, the Lord of the Universe, words that nobody before was given, from the beginning and the end of creation.

God endowed Moses with miracles and great signs that prove he was a Messenger of the Lord. Moses signs and miracles had been chosen to be compatible with the prevailing mentality of people of that time due to the propagation of witchcraft and charlatanism.

God ordained Moses to go to the Pharaoh and call on him to worship God, and to stop the oppression of people.

Moses fears the Pharaoh because he had killed a man and because they Pharaoh was also a tyrant. He was a tyrant who does not accept advice, especially when will be who invites him to submit to and worship God. The Pharaoh will surely refuse and kill anyone who would tell him this. God reassured Moses and says He is with him and watching him. He will protect him.

Mount Sinai is the holy mount where the **GREAT LORD GOD** spoke with the Prophet Moses in Egypt

(Image taken from Google Earth, September 2013)

The dialogue in this context has been stated in the Quran in the chapter Taha ((Go you and your brother, with my Signs and do not slacken in remembering Me. Go to Pharaoh, he has overstepped the bounds. But speak to him with gentle words so that hopefully he will pay heed or show some fear." They said "Our Lord, we are afraid that he might persecute us or overstep the bounds." He said," Have no fear I will be with you, All-Hearing and All-Seeing. Go to him and say," We are your Lord's Messengers so send the tribe of Israel away with us and do not punish them. We have brought you a Sign from your Lord. Peace be upon those who follow the guidance. It has been revealed to us that punishment is for him who denies the truth and turns away." Pharaoh said, "Who then is your Lord, Moses?" He said "Our Lord is He who gives each thing its created form then guides it." He said "What about the previous generations?" He said," Knowledge of them is with my Lord in a Book. My Lord does not misplace nor does He forget." It is He who made the earth a cradle for you and threaded pathways for you through it and sent down water from the sky by which we have brought forth various different types of plants. Eat and pasture your cattle. Certainly there are Signs in that for people of sound intellect. From it We created you, to it We will return you, and from it We will bring you forth a second time. We showed him all of Our Signs, but he denied and spurned them.)).

When Pharaoh had listened to Moses speech he became scared and shaken and cried "O Moses you and your brother are liars and clever magicians. You came to spread the terror and fear in the country by means of your magic and we will challenge you the same magic to show to people that you are merely a magician. You brought this magic to deracinate people from their land and propagate terror and fear. Moses if you are capable of defying our formidable magicians let us fix a time between us and you, so that people attending can see your magic and the cleverness of our magicians in challenging your skills." Moses agreed upon Pharaoh's proposal. The Pharaoh determined the time of the challenge and invited all subjects to attend this important event to see what will happen between Moses and Pharaoh's magicians. The time was fixed for the well-known festival day in the Pharaoh's kingdom, which is called "the day of festival." The Quran stated this interesting story related to Pharaoh's challenge of Moses, the facts of story has been cited in the chapter of the Taha ((He said, "Have you come to us to expel us from our land by means of your magic, Moses? We will bring you magic to match it. So fix a time between us and you which neither we nor you will fail to keep at a place where we can meet halfway." He said "your time is the day of the festival. The people should gather in the morning."))

The Pharaoh sent envoys to bring all magicians, charlatans and cassocks throughout all villages and towns of Egypt under the Pharaoh's rule. The magicians and charlatans answered the Pharaoh's appeal and order and they came to attend the meeting in presence of Pharaoh one day before the challenge with Moses (the Day of Festival).

Before the fixed time with Moses, the Pharaoh talked to him in presence of magicians and cassocks blaming him "O Moses, why these troubles against us while it is we who fostered you in our house since you was a boy and spent years of your age with us. Also you killed a man of us and you disappeared and you were among wrong doers. Moses replied "Yes I wronged in killing that man but I asked my Lord forgiveness and he forgave me. He is your Lord and Lord of the Universe. The Pharaoh mocked at Moses telling him, "Who is the Lord of the Universe?" Moses answered "He is the Lord of the universe and all it contains." The Pharaoh got angry and cried for the magicians and charlatans: "O people, do you hear this nonsense, Moses is a crazy person." The Pharaoh warned the audience against adoration of another god or the God of Moses rather than him. If they did, he will put them in jail and torture them. Moses seized the presence of all people and declared publicly that he is the Messenger of God. Pharaoh said: "What is your evidence, Moses?" Moses said: "God granted me a signs that prove the veracity of my words. Pharaoh! Look at mystaff, he threw it down and transformed in real fearsome snake moving at Moses order. Then Moses put his hand under his arm and emerged pure white light, and said to Pharaoh "You did not believe in Lord yet?" , Pharaoh said: "the time is the day of festival, and we will see if your magic is stronger than our magic." Pharaoh added " Moses is a clever magician."

Pharaoh gathered his magicians and promised them that if they defeat Moses, he will give them rewards and money. The magicians reassured the Pharaoh that they will win the challenge. This spectacle has been narrated within the dialogue between Moses and Pharaoh in presence of magicians in the chapter of Poets, God said ((Go to Pharaoh and say, "We are the Messenger of the Lord of all the worlds to tell you to send the tribe of Israel away with us." He said "Did we not bring you up among us as a child and did you not spend many years of your life among us? Yet you did the deed you did and were ungrateful." He said, "At the time I did it I was one of the misguided."))

((Pharaoh said "What is the Lord of all the worlds?" He said "The Lord of the heavens and the earth and everything between them if you knew for sure." He said "to those around him," Are you listening?" He said "Your Lord and the Lord of your forefathers, the previous peoples," He said, "the Messenger, who has been sent to you is mad." He said, "The Lord of the East and the West and everything between them if you used your intellect."

He said, "if you take any god other than me, I will certainly throw you into prison." He said "Even if I were to bring you something undeniable?" He said "Produce it then if you are someone telling the truth." So he threw down his staff and there it was, unmistakably a snake. And he drew out his hand and there it was, pure white to those who looked. He said to the High Council round about him, "This certainly is a skilled magician who desires by his magic to expel you from your land, so what do you recommend?" They said, "Detain him and his brother and send out marshals to the cities, to bring you all the skilled magicians." So the magicians were assembled for a meeting on a specified day. The people were asked," Are you all assembled so we can follow the magicians if they are the winners?" When the magicians came, they said to Pharaoh," Will we be rewarded if we are the winners?" He said "Yes, and in that case you will be among those brought near."))

People assembled in the fixed day "the day of festival" to see the magicians challenging Moses. Pharaoh was confident regarding the skillfulness of his magicians, but he knew deep down that there is extraordinary force behind Moses. Instead, he convinced himself of the strong ability of his magicians and hoped for the defeat of Moses.

The Day of Festival

People gathered, as agreed before with Moses and Pharaoh, in a grandiose festival. All people attended it in order to watch the strongest of magic fights between Moses and the Pharaoh magicians. The Pharaoh manifested in a ceremonial convoy, pleased among his troops, guards, entourage and slaves. He was confident of skills of his magicians as they promised him before and waited impatiently for the defeat of Moses.

Moses met the magicians and admonished them to fear and submit to God the Creator of everything and denounce their forbidden magic deeds. In fact, the speech of Moses impressed the magicians and some magicians was made sure of the authenticity of Moses. But they did not show their conviction by fear of Pharaoh oppression, and they all decided to enter in the challenge of magic with Moses. The Pharaoh gave order to start magic competition between Moses and his magicians. The magicians asked if he wanted to start first or them. Moses told them they could start first, they started their magic works by throwing their cords and staffs and concocted the magic effects which made people that these cords and staffs are moving snakes. These magic works amazed people and pharaoh as well, and he was delighted the performance of his magicians. He described them of great magic. Then they asked Moses to start.

Moses started his turn by mentioning the name of God and threw his staff down commanding it to swallow all what the magicians had thrown down. Moses staff swallowed up all cords and staffs of the magicians and their magic show foiled and frustrated owing to God's power that was put in the staff of Moses. As a result, the magicians were defeated, frustrated and ashamed. The Pharaoh was as well. Hence, the magicians agreed that Moses skills and miracles are not magic, but rather powers from God the Al-Mighty. They saw that this power was stronger than any magic or magician. As a result, the magicians declared their submission and belief regarding the genuineness of the Messenger Moses and his miracles.

The Pharaoh got extremely angry and menaced the magicians saying to them "Why do you believe in him? I will cut off your hands and your feet alternately." The magicians replied to him that they believed in Moses and Aaron's God and they are heedless of whatever he will do.

The Quran portrayed these impressive story of Moses victory against Pharaoh and his magicians and the victory of God's power over the disbelievers, as stated in the chapter of the Poets from the verse 37. ((They said detain him and his brother and send out marshals to the cities ,to bring you all the skilled magicians, So the magicians were assembled for a meeting on a specified day. The people were asked," Are you all assembled so we can follow the magicians if they are the winners?" When the magicians came, they said to Pharaoh, "Will we be rewarded if we are the winners?" He said, "Yes, and in that case you will be among those brought near." Moses said to them, "Throw whatever it is you are going to throw!" They threw down their ropes and staffs and said, "By the might of Pharaoh we are the winners." But Moses threw down his staff and at once it swallowed up what they had fabricated." The magicians threw themselves down, prostrating. They said, "We believed in the Lord of all the worlds, the Lord of Moses and Aaron." He said, "Have you believed in him before I authorized you? He is your chief who taught you magic. But you will soon know! I will cut off your alternate hands and feet and I will crucify every one of you." They said, "We do not care! We are returning to our Lord. We remain hopeful that our Lord will forgive us our mistakes for being the first of the believers."))

This event was a victory over Pharaoh and his magicians as also cited in Taha chapter, from verse 68. ((We said, "have no fear. You will have the upper hand. Throw down what is in your right hand. It will swallow down up their handiwork. Their handiwork is just a magician's trick. Magicians do not prosper wherever they go." The magicians threw themselves down in prostration. They said, "We believe in the Lord of Aaron and Moses." Pharaoh said, "Do you believe in him before I have authorized you? He is your chief, the one who taught you magic. I will cut off your hands and feet alternately and have you crucified on palm trunks. Then you will know for certain which of us has the harsher and longer lasting punishment."))

The Pharaoh and his troops decided to punish Moses and his Israelite followers and mobilized an army in order to eradicate them. God commanded Moses, his Israelite followers, and all others who believed in him to leave the city and head toward the sea. While they marched to the sea, the Pharaoh and his troops were tracking them to kill them all. When they reached the beach, the followers of Moses saw Pharaoh and his troops coming to besiege them. They had no escape – they were trapped. Moses followers panicked and said with fear, "What we will do? The Pharaoh and his troops are behind us and the sea is before us." Moses told them quietly and confidently that My Lord will guide me and tell me what to do. Moments later, God's order came to Moses telling him to hit the sea with his staff and a safe and dry path will be made on the sea. You and your followers have to cross within to other bank without fear. Pharaoh and his troops will soon follow you and they will be sunk in the sea at the time you are watching them. Moses hit the sea with his staff a dry path has been made for Moses and his followers crossed the sea to other bank. The Pharaoh and his troops followed them as God said they would, and when they reached the middle of path the sea returned to its initial nature and swallowed the Pharaoh and his troops. While the waters closed in on him, the Pharaoh voiced loudly "Now I believe in Moses's God."

This spectacle of Pharaoh sinking and the salvation of Moses and his followers has been portrayed in the Quran from the chapter of the Poets, from verse 60. ((So they pursued them towards the east. And when the two hosts came into sight of one another Moses companions said, "We will surely be overtaken!" He said, "Never, My Lord is with me and He will guide me." So He revealed to Moses, "strike the sea with your staff." And it split in two, each part like a towering cliff. And He brought the others right up to it. He rescued Moses and all those who were with him. Then He drowned the rest.))

The Quran stated Moses in numerous verses and his name cited 136 times in the Quran. Thus, it is the most repeated name in the Holy Quran and in every time the name of Moses is mentioned in the Quran, it is linked to an event and instruction for Moses and his companions and to those the Quran is sent down. Moses stories are part of divine law for Muslims, the proof on this is that during the first speech between God and Moses. He asked Moses to take off his sandals and this remained as a rule for Muslims forever. Once they enter worship place they take off their sandals outside. This rule is sent down to Moses and Muslims inherited it.

Moses is the second messenger after David. As cited in the Quran, his message was the Torah, God's Book sent down to Moses, which contained life's laws and worship jurisprudence in favor of the Israelite people and for others who follow him. As the human mind mutates, and his mental abilities develops over time, so does his conceptions and perceptions of things including the life hereafter and all spiritualties. Thus, the Messengers are sent according to each period in harmony with occurred mental and intellectual acuities of peoples.

Muslim religion has ordained Muslims to believe in Moses and Jesus, and it makes no difference between them and Prophet Mohammed, Islam's Messenger. Thus, the non–differentiation between the Torah, the Bible and the Quran is a part of Islamic faith and creed.

The disciples of Moses are supposed to respect and sanctify the Quran. In addition, Moses' disciples should know what is said about Moses in the Quran, and eventually they must respect and sanctify Islam's Messenger as observation of Moses Message.

Title: *Moses from Paint Crossing the Red Sea,*
by Bergamo

REFERENCE

The main reference of these book is the Islamic Holy Book, which is called **Quran Kareem**.

The Holy book of Muslim, the Quran, has been sent from Great Lord God to Mohamed (P.B. upon Him) through the Angel Gabriel.

The Quran Kareem consists of one hundred fourteen chapters (SORA) -- some of them are long chapters, and some of them are very small chapters. These chapters describe facts related to life and to the other world after death. Also mentioned are stories and facts about the old nations from Adam to Jesus to Mohamed. The Quran described and explained their life and behavior. Some chapters contain a description of the human future, and includes justice and laws to regulate the human life on earth.

A total of 25 prophets are mentioned in the Quran. Specific facts of each prophet have been mentioned to give a chance to us to know what happened to the people before us on earth. The prophets mentioned in Quran:-

Moses is mentioned 136 times in the Quran. Each mention of him talks about something different than the other. Abraham is mentioned 69 times -- each time is of different miracles and facts. Noah is mentioned 43 times, and Joseph is mentioned 27 times in Quran. Jesus is mentioned 25 times, as is Adam. Both are mentioned equally because both of them had been created differently than the other human. Isaac and Solomon were mentioned 17 times, while Jacob and David were mentioned 16 times. Ishmael 12 times, while Mohamed was mentioned in Quran only 4 times.

MOHAMED (Peace be upon Him)

MOHAMED was the son of Abdullah, and his grandfather Abduh Motaleb was from the Arabic tribe Koraish. Born in the city of Mecca, in Saudi Arabia in the year of AD 570. His father, Abdulah, died before he was born and his mother died while he was 2 years old. His childhood and youth have been documented in different references. He was quiet and honest. No one in his era recognized any mistakes by him.

In the age of forty he receive the message from God. He received the Quran and he was informed that he is a prophet, the last prophet on earth. And he will complete all other messages which came before him. Mohamed was illiterate. He didn't know how to read or write and that's the miracle he received from God. He was illiterate but he dictated this book, which was addressed to all humans.

Upcoming Books and Information

Mr. Ali Zwaik became an author for Deep Sea Publishing in 2013. This paperback book is also available for the Kindle and in EPUB formats for the Nook, iPad, and iPhone. Check into Deep Sea's website for more information on Mr. Zwaik, including book signing events and future releases.

Books and eBooks are available on www.amazon.com, www.barnesandnoble.com, and on Deep Sea's website shown below.

Deep Sea Publishing (DSP) is a Florida-based company that sells novels, young adult/teen fiction, children's books, photography books, and reference guides. The website mentioned below supplies details on all DSP publications and the expected release dates of new material.

www.deepseapublishing.com

www.ingramcontent.com/pod-product-compliance
Lightning Source LLC
LaVergne TN
LVHW010016070426
835511LV00001B/5